GARETH STEVENS
VITAL SCIENCE
Physical Science

FORCES AND MOTION

by Robert Snedden
Science curriculum consultant: Suzy Gazlay, M.A.,
science curriculum resource teacher

Please visit our Web site at: www.garethstevens.com
For a free color catalog describing Gareth Stevens Publishing's
list of high-quality books, call 1-800-542-2595 (USA) or
1-800-387-3178 (Canada).
Gareth Stevens Publishing's fax: 1-877-542-2596

Library of Congress Cataloging-in-Publication Data

Snedden, Robert.
 Forces and motion / Robert Snedden.
     p. cm. — (Gareth stevens vital science. Physical science)
 Includes bibliographical references and index.
 ISBN-13: 978-0-8368-8087-8 (lib. bdg.)
 ISBN-13: 978-0-8368-8096-0 (softcover)
 1. Force and energy. I. Title.
 QC73.S59   2006
 531'.6—dc22   2006033731

This edition first published in 2007 by
Gareth Stevens Publishing
A Weekly Reader® Company
1 Reader's Digest Rd.
Pleasantville, NY 10570-7000 USA

This edition copyright © 2007 by Gareth Stevens, Inc.

Produced by Discovery Books
Editors: Rebecca Hunter, Amy Bauman
Designer: Barry Dwyer
Photo researcher: Rachel Tisdale

Gareth Stevens editorial direction: Mark Sachner
Gareth Stevens editor: Carol Ryback
Gareth Stevens art direction: Tammy West
Gareth Stevens graphic design: Dave Kowalski
Gareth Stevens production: Jessica Morris and Robert Kraus

Illustrations by Stefan Chabluk, Keith Williams
Photo credits: CORBIS: pp. 18 (Ross Ressmeyer), 31 (Nawang Sherpa/Bogati.ZUMA); Getty Images:
pp. 15 (David Deas/DK Stock), 34 bottom (Imagno), 32 (Sasson Tiram/Israeli Tourism Ministry), 34 top
(Roger Viollet Collection); Istockphoto.com: pp. Cover (Mark Dietrich), 4 (Michael Palis), 6 (Bill Grove),
7 (Gregory Biggs), 8 (Tor Lindqvist), 10 (Ron Hilton), 12 (Benoit Rousseau), 13 (Nick Jones), 17 (Lisa
Eastman), title page & 20 (Hector Mandel), 24, 25 (Matthew Cole), 26 top (Jami Garrison), 26 bottom
(Randolph Pamphrey), 28 top (Rafa Irusta), 28 bottom (Burghard Drews), 29 (Robert Szczachor),
30 (Matthew Scherf), 36 (Ralf Hirsch), 37 (Joe Gough), 38 (Mark Tenniswood), 39 (Nicholas Rjabow),
40 (Antonio Harrison), 41 (Gianluca Camporesi), 42 (Jacom Stephens); Library of Congress: pp. 9, 11;
NASA: pp. 5, 16, 19, 21, 23; U.S. Air Force: p. 27; U.S. Navy: pp. 33 (Paul Farley, CIV), 35.

Printed in the United States of Ameica

2 3 4 5 6 7 8 9 10 10 09 08

TABLE OF CONTENTS

Words that appear in the glossary are printed in **boldface** type the first time they appear in the text.

Cover: A channel lock tool, an everyday example of a simple machine, can be used to crack a nut.

Title page: A skydiver's spread-eagle position helps slow the rate of descent.

Introduction

What is a force? Quite simply, forces are pushes and pulls. Forces are acting on us, and on everything around us all the time. Forces make things move, they make them change direction, they make them **speed** up and slow down, and they make them stop moving. If you push or pull something, if you stretch it or squeeze it, if you bend it or twist it, you are exerting a force.

Some forces act only when something actually touches something else. When you kick a ball, for example, you exert a force. Other forces, like **magnetism** and **gravity**, can act at a distance and make an object move without actually touching it.

Forces and Energy

What's the difference between force and **energy**? Energy makes things happen. Whenever anything happens, energy is transferred from one form to another. When a force acts on something, either pushing it or pulling it, it means that energy is being transferred. You can't apply a force unless you use energy. If you throw a ball, chemical energy stored in your arm muscles becomes **kinetic energy** (movement energy) in the ball.

Forces Are with You!

The effects of some forces are easy to see. If you accidentally knock a cup from the table,

you can see the force of gravity at work pulling it toward the ground. You can also see the force of its impact with the ground that causes it to break! To read this book, you need to exert a force on the pages with your

The climbers have to use the force of their muscles against the force of gravity to pull themselves up.

muscles to make them turn. If you swing a bat at a baseball, you can feel the force of the impact vibrating up your arms and see its effect as the ball accelerates away. With every step you take, you are pushing Earth away from you. With every breath, you are pulling air into your lungs.

Forces can act on invisibly small pieces of matter. Powerful forces, for example, hold together the tiny atoms that make up everything around us. Some forces are felt over great distances. The force of gravity acts right across the universe, shaping and holding together groups of planets, stars, and galaxies.

The billions of stars that make up this distant galaxy are held together by gravity's pull.

On the Move

You probably have a pretty good idea what is meant by motion. It has to do with movement. Of course to be able to say that something has moved, you have to be able to say where it started. This starting place is called the object's position. We can talk about the change in position in two ways. One is distance, which is the amount of ground covered by the object in its movement from one place to another. The second is **displacement**, which tells us how far the object is from its starting place. The two are not the same. Think about doing a lap of the running track. You run a distance of 400 yards (366 meters) but you end up back where you started from so your displacement is zero!

RISING APPLES

"I suppose that apples might start to rise tomorrow, but the possibility does not merit equal time in physics classrooms."

Stephen Jay Gould, paleontologist and historian of science (1941–2002)

CHAPTER 1

Speed and Acceleration

Speed is something we often talk about in everyday life. On the running track, you try to go faster than the other competitors, or if you play football, you might look for that extra burst of speed that will take you to the touchdown line. Many movies feature an exciting high-speed car chase; an aircraft needs to go fast enough to leave the ground for takeoff.

Speed

A commercial airliner at cruising altitude travels about 600 miles (966 kilometers) in an hour. That means, of course, that its speed is 600 miles (966 km) per hour. The definition of speed is this:

Speed = distance traveled/time taken

Usually this is written as:

$v = d/t$

where v = speed, d =distance traveled, and t = time.

A number of units can be used for measuring speed. In the airliner example, the speed is given as miles (km) per hour. We might also use inches per second (centimeters per second). The speedometer on a car might show speed in both miles and kilometers per hour. Highway patrol officers use **radar** devices that send out signals that bounce off an approaching vehicle. The radar device measures how long it takes for the signals to return to the radar, and that reveals the speed of the vehicle. The speed is displayed to the officer on a read out.

Speed on the football field is important if you want to dodge a tackle.

Average Speed

Suppose you make a journey in a car from your home to the store. Let's say that the store is 5 miles (8 km) away, and it takes fifteen minutes to get there. What was your speed? If you go 5 miles (8 km) in fifteen minutes, that's the same as going 20 miles (32 km) in an hour. At some points you were probably going faster than this, and maybe sometimes (such as when you were stuck at a stoplight) you weren't going anywhere. So 20 miles (32 km) per hour is the average speed of your journey.

Radar speed checks tell motorists if they are staying within the limit.

If you looked at the car's speedometer during the journey, you'd have seen it moving whenever the car's driver used the accelerator and brakes. The speedometer shows the speed of the car moment by moment. This is the **instantaneous speed**, the speed of the car at a particular instant. If the driver puts the car on cruise control, you would see **constant speed** as the car travels the same distance every second. The average speed for the journey is the total

SPEED OF LIGHT
Light is the fastest thing in the universe. It crosses the 93 million miles (150 million km) of space from the Sun to Earth in just 8.3 minutes at a speed of about 186,000 miles (300,000 km) per hour.

distance traveled divided by the amount of time it took to make the journey. Once again, it's $v = d/t$.

Velocity

We've been talking about the speed of things—the time it takes to cover a given distance. Sometimes it's important to know the direction a thing is going in as well as how fast it is traveling. For example, the space flight controllers in Houston, Texas, don't just need to know how fast the space shuttle is traveling. They need to know the direction in which it is going, too. This is important information because the space shuttle must climb at the correct angle to reach orbit.

The speed and direction of an object give us its **velocity**. Even more simply put: Velocity is speed in a particular direction. If you look at the car speedometer and see

Athletes accelerate down the track at the start of a 100-meter sprint.

40 miles (64 km) per hour, you know its speed. If you know what direction you are heading, you can determine the velocity, too. Finally, whenever your direction changes, your velocity changes, too— even if your speed remains the same.

Acceleration

Going back to the car journey, if the car's speed wasn't the same throughout the journey, then, pretty obviously, it must have been changing. The rate at which an object changes its velocity is called **acceleration**. An object is also accelerating if it changes direction. A car going around a bend at a constant speed is accelerating because its direction is changing even though its speed stays the same.

In the seventeenth century, Galileo Galilei carried out important experiments with acceleration. He rolled a ball down a long slope and carefully measured how the ball covered greater and greater distances in the same amount of time as it gathered speed down the slope. (Galileo didn't have a clock and used his own pulse to measure the time.) He discovered that the rate of acceleration of the ball was steady. This is called uniform acceleration.

Velocity-Time Graphs

One way of showing changing velocities over time is with a velocity/time graph. If you did one for an Olympic 100-meter sprinter, it might look like this:

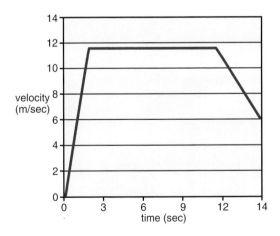

The sprinter accelerates to a top speed of just under 12 meters per second in about two seconds. The runner then maintains this speed for the rest of the race, slowing down only after crossing the finish line.

GALILEO GALILEI

Galileo Galilei (1564–1642) was born in Pisa, Italy. As a young man, he studied medicine at the University of Pisa but soon became interested in mathematics and **physics**. Specifically, he was curious about the way objects behaved when they moved. Through his studies, Galileo helped develop the modern scientific method. This method teaches that ideas can only be proved or disproved by careful experiment. Opinion and argument, Galileo believed, were not enough. He carried out many experiments with falling objects. One of the most famous showed that a light object and a heavy object both fell to Earth at the same rate. In 1609, using the newly invented telescope, he became the first person to see the four largest of Jupiter's moons (now called the "Galilean moons").

Newton's Laws

In the previous chapter, we defined acceleration as a change in something's velocity, either its speed or its direction. So, how do you change an object's velocity?

Right at the start, we said that a force was a push or a pull. To make something change direction, speed up, or slow down, it needs to be pushed or pulled. Sometimes it's a contact force that actually touches the object to get it moving. Sometimes it's a noncontact force, such as gravity or magnetism. This observation was first made

A freight train is a huge object. It takes a large force to get it moving or to stop it once it's rolling.

by Sir Isaac Newton, one of the most famous scientists the world has ever known. He explained it something like this:

> *An object at rest will stay at rest, and an object in motion will stay in motion at the same speed and in the same direction, unless it is acted upon by a force.*

We call this Newton's first **law** of motion. So a moving object will travel in a straight line at a constant speed unless

ISAAC NEWTON

British scientist Isaac Newton (1643–1727) spent most of his childhood with his grandmother because his father died before he was born. He attended Cambridge University but had to spend two years at home when the university was closed because of the plague. (This highly contagious disease swept through England and killed tens of thousands of people.) During this time, Newton studied the electromagnetic spectrum, invented the reflecting telescope (with which he observed the Moon and planets), and developed his laws of motion and gravity! Newton was a genius, but he was a hard man to get along with. He had many disagreements with his fellow scientists and hated to be criticized. Despite this, his achievements place him close to the top of the list of greatest scientists who ever lived.

a force acts on it, and a stationary object will remain stationary. This tendency that all objects have to remain at rest or in uniform motion is called **inertia**. The greater the **mass** of the object, the more inertia it has. Any force acting on the object has to overcome this inertia.

Newton also wondered how the size of the force applied to an object affected the rate at which it changed speed or direction. He answered that question with his second law of motion. This law says that a force acting on an object will cause the object to move in the direction of the force; the bigger the force, the greater will be the change of direction or speed. An object with a large mass needs a larger force than an object with a small mass to get it to

Did You Know

HIGH JUMPER
The acceleration rate of a jumping flea is twenty times faster than that of a launching space shuttle.

Forces and Motion

As long as the dogs all pull in the same direction, the sled will move smoothly and quickly across the snow.

accelerate at the same rate. Newton's second law explains why you can throw a 5-ounce (116-gram) baseball farther than a 10-pound (4.5-kilogram) rock.

One way of representing Newton's second law is like this: The greater the force acting on an object, the faster will be the change in its motion. In other words, the faster it will accelerate.

$$F = ma$$

where F = force, m = mass and a = acceleration

The unit of force is called the **newton**, in honor of Isaac Newton and his laws of motion. One newton is roughly the force needed to accelerate a mass of 2.2 pounds (1 kilogram) 3.281 feet (1 m) per second.

The force of the bat striking the ball will rapidly change its direction.

A baseball field is a good place to see Newton's laws in action. When the pitcher throws a ball toward a batter, he exerts a force that sets the ball in motion. If the batter makes contact with the ball, he will exert another force that will change the ball's direction and velocity. The first action illustrates Newton's first law: An object will stay still, or continue moving in the same direction at the same speed unless acted on by a force. The second action illustrates Newton's second law:

> *A force acting on an object will cause the object to move in the direction of the force.*

Where the ball goes depends on the angle it leaves the bat (the direction of the force) and how hard the bat hits it (the **magnitude** of the force).

SHUTTLE ACCELERATION

A fully fueled space shuttle on the launchpad weighs about 4.4 million pounds (2 million kilograms). A thrust of more than 36 million newtons is needed to overcome gravity and get the shuttle off the ground and into orbit. This thrust is provided by a combination of the main engines and the solid rocket boosters.

CHAPTER 3

Balanced and Unbalanced Forces

What happens when an object is acted on by more than one force at the same time, each one pulling or pushing in a different direction? Sometimes nothing seems to be happening at all. Think of two equally strong tug-of-war teams pulling against each other. Each team is pulling as hard as it can, so there are obviously forces at work, but the rope hardly moves. This is because the two forces are equal in magnitude but opposite in direction. They cancel each other out.

When two or more forces cancel each other out, we say that they are balanced, or in **equilibrium**. The object being acted on by these balanced forces does not change the way it is moving. And if it is at rest, it remains at rest.

Imagine that one of the tug-of-war teams weakens. When the force that team is exerting is lessened, the forces will no longer be in balance. The rope will start to move in the direction of the stronger pull of the other team. **Unbalanced forces** change the way an object moves. The unbalanced forces on the rope cause it to accelerate in the direction of the stronger pull.

The tug-of-war game is an example of the combined effect of opposing forces. Combined forces can also move in the same direction, such as several people pushing together to move a stalled automobile. If we want to know what

 **HOW ARE YOU AT MOVING EARTH?**

Did you know that every time you take a step you push Earth backward? Earth pushes against you with an equal and opposite force that propels you forward. Of course, Earth doesn't go back very far because it is so very much bigger than you are. The mass of Earth is roughly 13 quadrillion pounds (6 quadrillion kg), which is a lot more than you! Because Earth is so much bigger than you are, it really isn't going to move very much at all.

If the two teams in a tug-of-war are evenly balanced, the resultant force will be zero and there will be no movement either way.

will happen to an object with multiple forces acting on it, we have to take into consideration not only the magnitude of the forces, but also their direction. When we put together the effects of both magnitude and direction of forces, we get the **resultant force**. If the resultant force is zero, the forces are balanced.

Newton Again

Newton made another important discovery about forces: If you push something, it pushes you back just as hard as you are pushing but in the opposite direction. From this observation comes Newton's third law of motion. It states:

For every action, there is an equal and opposite reaction.

Newton's third law is in action all around us. If you are sitting in a chair as you read this book, you are pushing down on the chair, and the chair is pushing up on you, up with an equal but opposite force. The two forces are balanced so you neither sink through the chair nor shoot up into the air.

The space shuttle's engines produce colossal amounts of thrust to lift its mass against the force of gravity.

Putting Newton to Work

Before launch, the space shuttle stays on the launchpad because of Newton's first law. The forces acting on it are in balance. According to Newton, unless an unbalancing force acts on it, the shuttle will remain "an object at rest." It will stay stuck on the launchpad. So why does the shuttle off the ground when the engines fire?

Inside the **combustion chamber** of the rocket engine, **propellants** are burned. When this happens, gases at very high temperatures are produced. The particles that make up these gases have a lot of energy and are moving very fast. Inside the combustion chamber, they push against the walls in all directions. If the chamber were sealed, the push of the gas particles would balance, and the rocket would not move. However, the combustion gases can actually escape through a bell-shaped nozzle at the rear of the rocket. The forces inside the chamber are now unbalanced. The push of the gases on the chamber is now greater in the forward direction. The result is that the rocket accelerates in the direction of the push.

The rocket is obeying Newton's third law. The gases escaping from the nozzle are the action, and the forward push, or thrust, is the reaction. The force of the gases rushing out is the same magnitude as the force thrusting the rocket forward. The same principle applies when you blow up a balloon and then let it go to fly around the room. The air rushing from the balloon's neck propels the balloon in the opposite direction.

So what determines how fast the rocket accelerates? Newton has the answer again, but this time it's the second law. Because force equals mass times acceleration, if we want to produce a large force, we need to have a large mass being accelerated as much as possible. Or in other words, the more rocket fuel burned, the hotter, and therefore, faster-moving will be the gas produced. As a result, the thrust will be greater.

Another thing to remember is that the mass of the shuttle decreases as the

fuel is used up, but the thrust stays the same as long as the engines continue to fire. So the rate of acceleration increases until the solid rocket boosters run out of fuel two minutes after launch. By this time, the shuttle is 28 miles (45 km) up and traveling at about 3,000 miles (5,000 km) per hour. That's pretty good going from a standing start!

When you kick off on your skateboard, you actually push the whole world back—but it's just a very tiny amount!

Gravity

There is one force that we all feel, all of the time. It is the pull of Earth. This pull is what makes an apple fall to the ground, and it's what makes you weigh what you do. This pull is the force of gravity—a force of attraction that exists between all objects that have mass.

Another of Isaac Newton's great achievements was the realization that the force that makes the apple fall is the same force that keeps the Moon in orbit around Earth. He called it the gravitational force.

Every single thing in the universe produces a gravitational force that attracts everything else. If you stand beside your friend, you are being attracted to each other by gravity. The larger the mass of an object, the greater the gravitational force it will produce. The force of attraction between you and your friend is

FUNDAMENTAL FORCES

Gravity is one of the four fundamental, or universal, forces because it is something that affects every single mass in the universe, from atoms to galaxies. Two of the other **fundamental forces** are the strong nuclear force, which hold together atoms, and the weak nuclear force, which causes radioactivity. These operate on minute distance scales at the level of atoms. The fourth fundamental force is the **electromagnetic force**, which is the force between atoms and molecules. The electromagnetic force arises from the fact that particles can have a positive or a negative charge and either pull together if their charges are different or push apart if their charges are the same. It is responsible for electricity and magnetism.

Particles on the cat's fur have an opposite electrical charge to particles on the balloon. This results in a force of attraction that pulls the cat's fur up.

so small compared to the big pull of Earth's gravity that it isn't noticeable.

Newton published a law of universal gravitation that showed how to calculate this force. It says that the force of gravity between two objects depends on the mass of the objects and their distance apart. Gravity becomes weaker as the distance between the objects increases.

Weighty Matters

Sometimes the gravitational force is referred to by a simple everyday term—**weight**. The weight of an object is really a way of measuring how strongly the force of gravity

An astronaut on the Moon weighs only a sixth of what he does on Earth–but he hasn't lost any mass.

is pulling on it. Everything has mass, which is the amount of material it contains. The more massive an object, the more the force of gravity pulls on it, and the heavier, or weightier, it is.

There are three ways to change an object's weight. You can take some of its mass away and make it lighter. You can add mass to it and make it heavier. Or, you can move it to a place that is bigger or smaller than Earth. If you could stand on Jupiter, you'd weigh three times what you do on

Earth. If you went to Mars, however, you'd only weigh one-third as much. On the Moon you'd weigh one-sixth of what you do on Earth, which is why the astronauts who went there were able to hop around like kangaroos.

Terminal Velocity

An object falling through the air is being affected by another force in addition to gravity. This force is called **air resistance**, or **drag** force. It is caused by **friction** between the falling object and the particles in the air. The size of the drag force depends on the shape of the object. A smooth, **streamlined** object has less drag.

The faster the object is going, the greater the drag force. This means that the faster an object is falling, the greater is the drag force on it. As a falling object accelerates under gravity, its drag force increases. The net effect of this is that as the drag increases, the acceleration decreases at an equal rate. Eventually, the drag force exactly matches the force of gravity. The object continues to fall, but it will not accelerate any more. At this point, it is said to have reached its **terminal velocity.**

Terminal velocity for a skydiver is between 93 and 124 miles (150 and 200 km) per hour. It would not be a good idea to hit the ground at this speed. Opening a parachute increases the drag force, which helps overcome the force of gravity. This

When the drag force caused by air resistance matches the pulling force of gravity, the skydiver is no longer accelerating downward. He or she has reached terminal velocity.

means that the skydiver slows down. Slowing down decreases the drag force, and eventually the skydiver reaches a new terminal velocity that is slow enough to allow a safe landing.

Gravity on a Grand Scale

The force of gravity determines the paths of the planets and all other objects through space. The Moon stays in orbit around Earth and Earth stays in orbit around the Sun because of gravity. It is also because of gravity that very large objects such as stars or planets are spherical. Anything larger than 250 miles (400 km) in diameter has such a powerful **gravitational field** that the rocks will flow like a very slow-moving liquid. Over time, everything is pulled in toward the center of gravity of a planet or star, and it takes the form of a sphere. This is because every part of a sphere's surface is an equal distance from the center.

Projectile Motion

You'll remember that an object travels in a straight line at a constant speed unless a

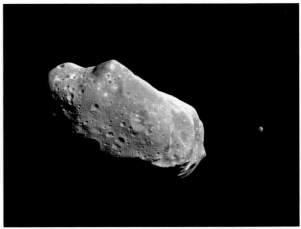

This is the irregularly shaped asteroid Ida. Its gravity isn't strong enough to pull it into a sphere, but it is strong enough to hold the small object on the right in orbit around it.

force acts upon it. If a force acts on the moving object to make it change direction, the object will follow a curved path. Imagine throwing a football. The football doesn't follow a straight path through the air. It follows a curved path because of the force of gravity pulling on it at right angles to the direction in which you threw it. The movement of an object that has been thrown, or propelled, but no longer has any contact force being applied to it, is called **projectile motion**.

Did You Know?

CENTER OF GRAVITY

Earth and the Moon orbit around their common center of gravity, which is located 1,000 miles (1,600 km) beneath the surface of Earth. The center of Earth makes a small circle around that center of gravity every 27.3 days.

Falling around Earth

Gravity pulls all objects equally. A cannonball fired from a cannon that is parallel to the ground will hit the ground at the same time as a similar cannonball that is simply dropped from the same height. This is because the only force acting on each cannonball is the force of gravity pulling each cannonball toward Earth. The cannonball fired from the cannon will land farther away of course! The greater the force propelling the cannonball from the cannon, the farther away it will fall.

Just like the thrown football, the cannonball follows a curved path. Imagine you have a cannon on top of a high mountain and you fire a cannonball from it with great force (see diagram above). The cannonball falls toward the ground on a curved path as before (ball A). The faster it goes the further it goes (balls B and C). Because the surface of Earth is also curved, if the cannonball is going fast enough, its curved path will follow the curve of Earth (ball D). It will still be falling, but it will stay at the same height and won't reach the ground. The cannonball will have become a satellite.

Of course, the cannonball would be slowed down by air resistance and would eventually fall to Earth. It would also have to be going very, very fast to stay in orbit at such a low altitude.

Feeling Weightless

Astronauts in orbit feel weightless, but they aren't really. They would have to be much farther away from Earth not to feel the

WHAT ARE GEOSTATIONARY ORBITS?

A satellite in airless space has no air resistance to slow it down. The velocity of the space shuttle in orbit 186 miles (300 km) above Earth is roughly 17,400 mph (28,000 km/h). Many communications satellites are in what are called geostationary orbits. This means that they appear to stay in position above the same spot on Earth's surface. The reason they can do this is that they take exactly the same time to orbit Earth as Earth does to turn beneath them. A geostationary satellite orbits 22,300 miles (35,800 km) above Earth, at an orbital speed of around 7,000 miles (11,000 km) per hour.

effects of its gravity. The spacecraft, and everything in it, including the astronauts, feel weightless because everything in orbit is in a constant state of free fall around Earth. This results in a feeling of **weightlessness**.

Centripetal Force

The propeller on an aircraft, the wheels on your bike, and the CD spinning in your stereo system are all turning in circles. How is it possible to get circular motion from straight-line forces? Well, as we've seen, a thrown football and an orbiting satellite both follow curved paths because of the force of gravity acting upon them. A spinning object is also constantly changing direction. A turning force, whether it's from your feet on the pedals or the engine in the aircraft, sets the object in motion. The resultant force acts toward the center of the circle, pulling the wheel (or propeller or CD) in toward its center. Because this force is always at right angles (perpendicular) to the direction of motion, it has no effect on the object's velocity, but it is constantly changing the direction. This force is called the **centripetal force**. For the orbiting satellite, the centripetal force is gravity.

These astronauts are not really weightless. As long as they stay in orbit, they, their equipment, and the space station are all in continual free fall around Earth.

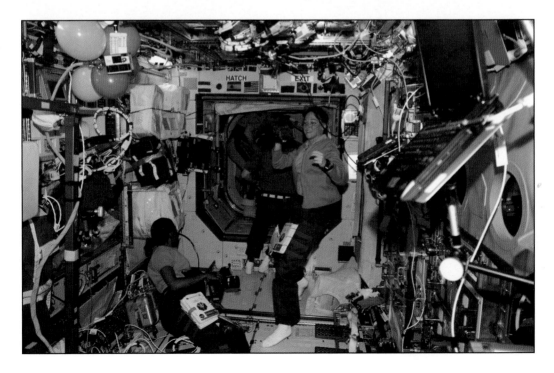

CHAPTER 5

Friction

Friction occurs where a moving object rubs against a surface or against another moving object. It is the force that causes objects to slow down and come to a stop. Friction is present whenever anything moves on Earth, and it acts against the direction of motion. When a rolling ball slows down and comes to a stop, it's because friction is acting on it. Otherwise—according to Newton's first law—it would just keep rolling.

The amount of friction between two surfaces depends on the surface textures and on how strong the force is pressing them together. The harder you push two surfaces together, the greater the friction between them will be. The rougher the surfaces are, the greater the friction will be.

Friction is what makes it hard to drag a heavy object over a rough surface.

The shape of an object can affect friction. The smaller the areas of the surfaces that are touching, the less the friction will be. A ball or a wheel rolls along easily because only a small part of the

Tractors need tires with very deep treads so that they have good **traction** on steep slopes and muddy fields.

Bike tires both make use of and reduce friction. The small area of the tire touching the ground reduces friction, but at the same time the tires grip the surface, giving traction.

surface touches the ground at any time. A solid block of rubber being pushed along the ground wouldn't move nearly as easily as the rubber tire on your bike. The block would have much more rubber surface touching the ground and therefore would experience more friction.

There are different types of friction. The type that slows objects that are already in motion is called kinetic friction, or sliding friction. Another type is static friction,

which happens when a motionless object resists being pulled or pushed across a surface. Static friction has to be overcome for the object to be set in motion.

We have already come across another type of friction. This is fluid friction, or drag, the friction between an object and a gas or liquid. Air resistance is a type of fluid friction. It is also fluid friction that makes it a lot harder to wade through water than to walk across dry land.

STREAMLINING HELPS
A racing cyclist often pushes aside 1 ton (.907 tonne) of air every minute. It helps to be streamlined!

Reducing Friction

Friction is one of the main ways in which energy is lost in machines. It converts kinetic energy into heat energy, which can't be used to do any useful work. About one-fifth of the energy used by an

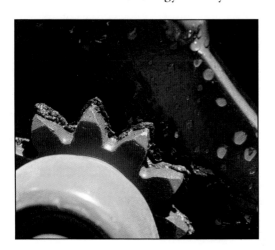

The thin blades of the hockey player's skates keep friction to a minimum so he moves quickly across the ice.

automobile is simply lost as friction between the moving parts.

One way to reduce friction is to use highly polished surfaces. But even the smoothest of surfaces is covered in microscopic bumps and dents. There is always some friction as the bumps of one surface get caught in the dents of another.

Lubrication is another way of cutting down friction. A thin layer of oil, grease, or other suitable substance is used to separate the surfaces so they don't actually touch

Oil is used to reduce friction between moving metal machinery parts.

each other. For instance, good lubrication is essential to keep an automobile moving smoothly. The suspension, steering, gears, and engine are all kept well lubricated with oil or grease. Ice skates are another good example. They are designed to reduce friction in two ways. First, they have a very small area in contact with the ice. Second, the **pressure** of the skates on the ice partially melts it, so there is a very thin layer of lubricating liquid water between the ice and the skate.

Shape also plays a role in reducing friction. Many water-living animals, such as fish and dolphins, are streamlined to cut through the water with the least possible **resistance**. Cars and aircraft are streamlined, too. Many vehicle shapes are designed to reduce air resistance to the least amount possible. This makes them more fuel-efficient because less energy is lost pushing them through the air.

Useful Friction

Friction isn't all bad. In fact, we'd have a hard time without it. Imagine if every time you picked up something to eat, it slipped straight through your fingers. Imagine if every step you took was like walking on slippery ice. Imagine if you put on the brakes on your bike and nothing happened. Imagine if the car tires didn't grip the road at all. As you can see, life without friction would be challenging.

The Nighthawk deploys a small parachute as it lands. Air resistance acting on the chute brings the aircraft to a fast halt.

CHAPTER 6

The Pressure Is On

Try pushing your finger into a cork bulletin board. Now try pushing a thumbtack into the board. The thumbtack goes in easily, but your finger doesn't, even though you probably used about the same amount of force each time. Why should that be? The answer has to do with pressure.

It takes a lot less effort to push a thumbtack into a bulletin board than it would take to push your finger in!

Pressure is a measure of the amount of force applied over an area. It is measured in newtons per square meter (N/m^2). Another name for newton per square meter is pascal, named after the French scientist Blaise Pascal, who studied air pressure.

So how does pressure explain the thumbtack and the finger? The point of the thumbtack has a much smaller area than the tip of your finger, but the pressure exerted on the board by the thumbtack is much greater than that exerted by your finger. When you push on the thumbtack, the force is concentrated into the small area of the tip of the thumbtack.

Snowshoes and Camels' Feet

Sometimes, it's a good idea to reduce pressure. Snowshoes offer a good example. In places that have heavy snowfalls in winter, you might see people walking around in snowshoes. The snowshoe spreads out your weight over a larger area than your foot, which reduces the pressure on the snow. You

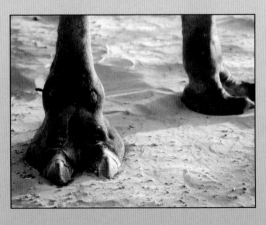

The big feet of the camel spread out, helping to prevent it from sinking into the soft sand.

Snowshoes increase the surface area of the walker that is in contact with the snow. This reduces the pressure that would make him or her sink into the snow.

don't sink as far into the snow as you would otherwise. A camel has big, flat feet for much the same reason. The weight of its body is spread over a large area so the camel doesn't sink into the sand of the desert as it walks.

If you're ever unlucky enough to find yourself sinking into a swamp or quicksand, the best thing to do is to throw yourself flat. This increases the area of your body in contact with the quicksand and so reduces the pressure that is making you sink into it.

Air Pressure

We are bombarded by trillions of air molecules every second. The force of all these collisions is what we call air pressure, and it is a powerful force. The pressure exerted by the atmosphere is measured in pounds per square inch, or psi. At sea level, the air pressure is 14.7 psi (1.03 kilogram-force per square centimeter, or kgf/cm^2). The reason this pressure does not crush us is that there is an equal pressure from inside our bodies keeping the forces in balance.

When you blow up a balloon, you are making the air pressure inside the balloon greater than the pressure outside. The molecules of air inside the balloon move around rapidly, striking the inside of the balloon. Every time a particle strikes the balloon, it pushes it out. Molecules in the air outside are striking the balloon, too, but not as often. As a result, the force of the impacts pushing out is greater than the force of the impacts pushing in, so the balloon expands.

Have you ever taken a drink through a straw? Did you know that you weren't actually sucking the liquid up by yourself? When you suck on the straw, you are drawing air out from it and so reducing the pressure in the straw. **Atmospheric pressure** on the liquid in your bottle or glass pushes it up through the straw and into your mouth.

Measuring Pressure

One way of measuring air pressure is by using a **barometer**. Italian scientist Evangelista Torricelli discovered the principle of the barometer in 1645. He turned a slim tube of glass, sealed at one

The air pressure inside the balloons is greater than the pressure outside. That is what keeps them inflated.

Air pressure on a mountaintop is much lower than it is at sea level.

end, upside down in a container of liquid. He discovered that the pressure of the air pushing down on the liquid forced it up into the tube. He could then measure the atmospheric pressure by measuring how far the liquid went up the tube.

As the air pressure varies from day to day according to the weather, the height of the liquid in the tube rises and falls.

Have you ever noticed how the pressure on your ears increases when you dive to the bottom of a pool? The deeper the water, the greater the pressure. The increased pressure is due to the weight of all the water above you. The same is true with air pressure—it's greater at sea level than it is up in the mountains. A quick change in altitude might make your ears pop! When the pressure on the tubes inside your ears changes, your eardrums may bend or move quickly. The motion may translate in your brain as a popping sound.

Water Pressure and Buoyancy

Pressure in a liquid acts in all directions. A fish in the sea has pressure on all parts of its body, from left and right and from above and below.

The upward push of a liquid on something is called **buoyant force**. This force affects all objects in a liquid, not just the ones that float. If you lie in the bathtub and lift your leg out of the water, do you notice that it feels lighter in the water than

The salty water of the Dead Sea in the Jordan Rift Valley keeps this swimmer afloat with its buoyant force.

out of it? This is because the buoyant force of the water supports part of your leg's weight. All liquids exert a buoyant force. The reason for this is that the pressure inside the liquid increases as the depth of the liquid increases. The pressure on the bottom of the object is greater than the pressure on the top, so the resultant buoyant force is upward. Of course, there is also a downward force due to gravity. If the buoyant force is greater than the force of gravity, the object will float.

Archimedes' Principle

According to Archimedes' principle, the weight of fluid displaced by an object in the fluid is equal to the buoyant force on that

When a submarine is about to dive, it floods its ballast tanks to increase its density— so it sinks. To come to the surface again the water is pumped back out of the tanks.

object. If the weight of water displaced is equal to the weight of the object, the object will float. The weight of the fluid depends entirely upon its **density** and the **volume** displaced.

Legend has it that the Greek mathematician Archimedes, who lived over two thousand years ago, discovered this while taking a bath. He noticed that the more of him there was in the water, the more the water level rose as he displaced it. He was so excited that he leaped from his bath and ran through the streets shouting,

Archimedes (c.287–212 B.C.) was one of the greatest mathematicians and thinkers of the ancient world.

"Eureka!" (which in Greek means "I have found it!")

Whether or not an object floats or sinks depends not on its weight but on its density. Density measures the amount of material in a given volume. One pound or kilogram of wood takes up more space than the same amount of iron because the wood is much less dense than the iron.

Liquids also have density. If an object placed in a liquid has the same density as the liquid, it will be neutrally buoyant and will neither sink nor float. If the object is less dense than the liquid, the buoyant

BLAISE PASCAL

Blaise Pascal (1623–1662) was born in the town of Clermont Ferrand, France. His mother died when he was four, and he was brought up by his two older sisters. He astonished his father with the speed of his learning. Pascal never enjoyed good health but still worked intensely, particularly at mathematics. Before he was sixteen, he had proved complex theories in geometry. At nineteen, he invented one of the first mechanical adding machines. Pascal also did a lot of work with barometers, used for measuring air pressure. With the help of his brother-in-law, he proved that air pressure decreases with altitude. He spent most of the last years of his life devoted to religious writings and died in Paris, France.

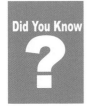

Did You Know?

DEEPEST OCEAN
The pressure at the bottom of the Challenger Deep, the deepest part of the Pacific Ocean (in the western Pacific near the island of Guam), is 16,000 pounds per square inch (1,120 kg/m^2). This is the equivalent weight of fifty jumbo jets!

force will be enough to send it to the surface. If the object is denser than the liquid, the buoyant force will not support it, and it will sink.

So if iron is denser than water, why does a ship float? If it were made of solid metal the ship would sink. However, a ship is full of air spaces, which effectively reduce its density. Its volume is much bigger than it would be if it were solid, so it displaces a greater amount of water. Because the overall density of the ship is less than the density of the water it displaces, the ship floats.

An aircraft carrier weighs thousands of tons (tonnes), yet it floats because it is full of air-filled spaces that reduce its density.

Squashing and Stretching

What actually happens to an object when a force acts on it? We've seen that forces make things start to move or change direction or speed up or slow down. But forces can have another effect, too. Depending on the nature of the object and the force acting on it, the force may actually change the shape of the object. Some things will stay out of shape, but others will return to the way they were, once the force is no longer being applied.

Clay changes shape readily when a force is applied to it.

Mechanical Properties

Mechanics deals with objects in motion and the forces acting upon them. A force that acts on an object and changes its shape is called a **stress**. The amount by which the object changes shape is called the **strain**. The higher the stress, the greater the strain will be.

Knowing the mechanical properties of materials, which tell us how they will behave when forces act on them, is important when it comes to choosing which materials to use for a particular purpose. Some of the most important mechanical properties of materials are stiffness, toughness, strength, resistance to stress, and **elasticity**.

The bow and bowstring have high elasticity. They will spring rapidly back to their original shapes when the archer releases the arrow.

Stiffness

The stiffness of a material determines how much it will bend when a force acts on it. For example, it wouldn't be a good idea to make shelves of rubber, because they'd bend alarmingly whenever any weight was placed in them. Rubber is good for car tires, however, because it is a strong, flexible material.

Toughness and Strength

Toughness measures how resistant a material is to cracking when it is placed under stress. The strength of a material is a measure of how great a force can act on it without breaking it. A material's strength depends on several factors, including its toughness and its shape.

Resistance to Stress and Elasticity

Some materials, such as clay and rubber, don't resist stress and change their shape very easily. Some materials will return to their original shape as soon as the stress is removed. The ability of an object to return to its original size and shape after being squeezed or stretched by a force is called **elasticity**. Some materials are more elastic than others. If you stretch out a rubber band and let it go, it regains its shape quickly. Other materials, such as glass, don't change shape very easily at all. They are brittle and break.

Forces and Motion

No matter how elastic a material is, it can't be stretched forever. Eventually there comes a point when the material will either snap or just not return to its original shape. When this happens, it is said to have passed its **elastic limit**.

When you apply a force to compress a spring or to stretch a rubber band, you are transferring energy into the spring or band. This is called **elastic potential energy**. As soon as the spring or band can return to its original shape, this energy will be released.

Elastic Sports

Elastic potential energy is important in sports. When a tennis ball hits the strings of a racket, the ball is squashed nearly flat by the force of the impact. For just a

The elastic energy stored in the trampoline propels the jumper high in the air as it springs back into shape.

fraction of a second, elastic potential energy is stored in the ball and also in the racket strings, which are stretched by the force. As ball and racket spring back into shape, the release of energy helps speed the ball on its way.

A pole-vaulter's pole is actually a complex piece of equipment. It is made from a lightweight and flexible **composite** of carbon fiber and fiberglass. The pole-vaulter runs as fast as he or she can to get the maximum kinetic energy. As the vaulter plants the pole and begins to vault upward, the pole bends, storing the kinetic energy as elastic potential energy. As it springs back into shape, the pole releases this energy and propels the vaulter over the bar.

BASEBALL FORCES

It might surprise you to know that a professional baseball player can apply a force of more than 40,000 newtons to a baseball. This is enough to distort the baseball to half its normal size, decelerate it from its pitched speed of about 90 miles (140 km) per hour to zero and accelerate it to more than 100 miles (160 km) per hour and send it on its way to the bleachers. All of this occurs in about a thousandth of a second!

Machines

Machines help us change energy from one form to another. Machines make our lives much easier because they allow us to do things that we'd find difficult or impossible to accomplish by muscle power alone. Simple machines magnify or direct a force from one place to another. A force, called the effort, is applied at one part of the machine. This moves another part of the machine that overcomes a resisting force, called the load.

Some machines work better, or more efficiently, than others. The measurement of the efficiency of a machine is called its mechanical advantage—the number of times a machine increases the amount of force put into it.

The Inclined Plane

A machine can be a very simple thing. The **inclined plane** is nothing more than a slope or ramp, but it is an example of a force magnifier. It takes less energy to lift an object to a higher level by pushing it along an inclined plane than to lift it vertically. The object being raised moves further along the ramp, but less force is used to reach the top of the ramp than it would take to lift it straight up. Just think how much easier it is to climb stairs than it would be to haul yourself vertically up a rope! The shallower the angle of the ramp, the less effort is needed to push something up it, but the greater the distance you have to go.

The Wedge

A wedge is a simple machine that is used to separate two objects or to remove a part of an object. It is really two moveable

An ax is a wedge on the move, splitting the logs in two.

A drill bit is like a spiraling inclined plane with a wedge at the cutting edge.

inclined planes stuck back to back. As a wedge pushes against an object, the pressure from its pointed shape adds force to the energy that was used to strike the object with the wedge. An ax, for example, can split logs with little effort.

The Screw

A screw is another kind of simple machine. It is a form of inclined plane. Think of the thread of the screw as being like a ramp with a wedge at the beginning going around the central shaft of the screw.

Turning the screw makes it move backward or forward just like going up and down a ramp. The closer together the threads of the screw, the less the slope of the ramp. A screw with close threads turns with less effort, but you will need to turn it many times to tighten it.

The Lever

The **lever** is one of the most common simple machines. A lever is used to apply a force to an object that can turn freely around a fixed point. This point is called a pivot or **fulcrum**. The force applied to a lever is called the effort force, and the force produced is called the load force. You can use a lever to lift things up or to turn things around.

There are three different classes of lever:

- A *first-class lever* (see below) has the fulcrum between the effort and the load. It multiplies the force applied to it.

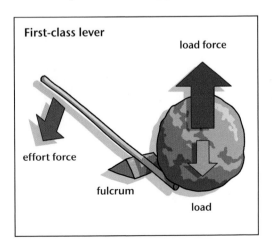

First-class lever

load force

effort force

fulcrum

load

- A *second-class lever* has the load between the effort and the fulcrum. A wheelbarrow is an example of a second-class lever. The load is in the barrow, the effort comes from pushing on the barrow, and the fulcrum, or pivot, is the barrow's wheel. Like the first-class lever, this lever is also a force multiplier.

- A *third-class lever* magnifies distance rather than force. An example of this would be a fishing rod. A fairly small flick of the wrist becomes a large movement at the end of the rod. Your wrist in this case is the fulcrum, and the fishing rod is a third-class lever in action.

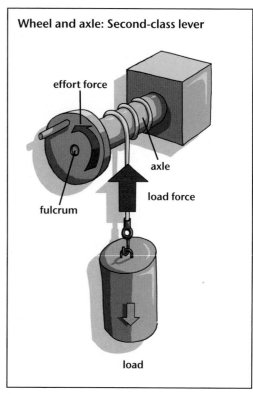

Wheel and axle: Second-class lever

effort force

axle

load force

fulcrum

load

The Wheel and Axle

The wheel and **axle** can be used in two different ways. The first way is as a rotating lever where the axle turns around the fulcrum of the lever (see above). Both the steering wheel of a car and a doorknob are like this. The driver's hands on the wheel cause the shaft, which is the axle in this case, to turn and so operate the steering mechanism of the car. A screwdriver is also a wheel and axle, with the handle of the screwdriver taking the place of the wheel.

The fishing rod is a third-class lever. The tip of the rod magnifies the movement of the wrist.

ARCHIMEDES

**"Give me but one firm
spot on which to
stand, and I will
move the Earth."**

Archimedes (c287–211 B.C.),
on the action of levers

The second way to use a wheel and axle is by using the wheel to cut down friction when you are moving something. When you pedal your bike, the bicycle chain turns the rear wheel's axle. The rim of the wheel turns with less force but travels a greater distance. As only the bottom part of the wheel is touching the ground at any time, friction is kept to a minimum with the result that you speed along.

The Pulley

A **pulley** is like a wheel and axle, but with a rope attached that runs through a groove in the rim of the wheel. Pulling down on the rope moves the load on the other end upward. The amount that the pulley reduces the effort needed to move the load depends on the number of pulley wheels used. A single-wheeled pulley does no more than change the direction of the force being applied. With a block-and-tackle system, which has two pulley wheels at each end (see right), the same effort will lift four times the weight but only one-quarter of

the distance. Pulleys are excellent machines for moving heavy weights around because they can be made with a high mechanical advantage—that is, they greatly multiply the amount of effort put into them. By using a system of pulleys, you could lift many times the amount of weight that you could move otherwise. Cranes use a system of pulleys to lift large objects.

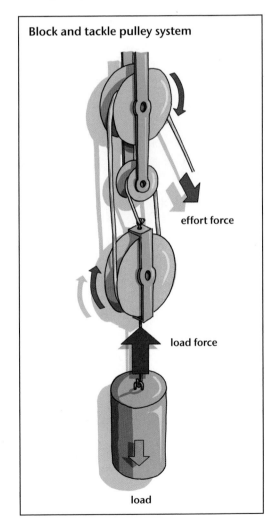

Block and tackle pulley system

effort force

load force

load

acceleration the rate at which velocity changes

air resistance a form of friction caused by collisions between air molecules and an object moving through the air

atmospheric pressure the force of the atmosphere pushing down

axle a shaft on which a wheel or pair of wheels revolves

ballast a heavy substance used to improve the stability of ships

barometer a device for measuring atmospheric pressure

buoyant force the upward push of a liquid on an object

centripetal force an inward pulling force that keeps an object moving in a circular path

combustion chamber the place in a rocket engine where the burning of fuel occurs

composite a material made of two or more substances

constant speed traveling at a steady speed, neither getting faster nor slowing down

density a measure of the amount of mass contained within a unit of volume

displacement the difference between the starting position of something and a later position

drag a frictional force that slows down an object moving through a liquid or gas

effort the force applied to part of a simple machine, such as a lever, to do work

elastic limit the point beyond which any further stretching of an object will result in it being unable to return to its original shape

elastic potential energy energy stored in a stretched or compressed object that is released when the object returns to its original shape

elasticity the ability of a material to regain its original shape after being stretched or compressed

electromagnetic force the force between atoms and molecules resulting from them having a positive or negative electric charge

energy the ability to make something happen; whenever anything happens energy is changing from one form into another

equilibrium a state in which all the forces acting on an object are in balance and the resultant force is zero

force a push or pull

friction a force that resists motion between two objects in contact with each other

fulcrum a point or support around which something turns

fundamental forces the basic forces of the Universe that affect all of the matter in it

gravitational field the region of space across which an object exerts a force of gravity

gravity a force of attraction between bodies of matter

inclined plane a slope or ramp

inertia the tendency of an object to remain at rest or to keep moving in a straight line unless acted upon by a force

instantaneous speed the speed of an object at a particular moment of time

kinetic energy the energy of a moving object

law in science, a rule that tells you what will happen in a particular set of circumstances; for example Newton's Laws of Motion describe the behavior of moving objects

lever a rigid piece that transmits and modifies force

load the resisting force that is overcome by the effort force applied in a simple machine

lubrication the use of oil or grease to reduce friction between moving parts

magnetism a non-contact force that acts on certain materials such as iron

magnitude a measure of the size of something, such as a force

mass the amount of material or matter that makes up an object

mechanics the study of the effects of forces on objects

newton the unit of force

pressure a measure of a force acting over a given area

projectile motion the movement of an object that has been thrown but no longer has contact force being applied to it

propellant fuel used by a rocket engine

pulley a wheel with a rope attached that runs through a groove

radar a way of discovering the position of something using radio signals

resistance an opposing force

resultant force the net force produced by combining two or more forces

speed the rate at which an object moves

strain the amount by which an object changes shape when acted on by a stress

streamlined shaped to cut through air or water with the least resistance

stress a force that acts on an object and changes it shape

terminal velocity the velocity reached by an object falling through air when the resistant force of the air is equal to the force of gravity

traction the adhesive friction of a body on a surface on which it moves

unbalanced force the resultant force when the forces acting on an object are not in equilibrium

velocity the speed and direction of an object

volume the amount of space something occupies

weight a measure of the force of gravity acting on an object

weightlessness the experience of objects in freefall apparently having no weight

Books

Forces and Gravity.
Discovery Channel School Science (series)
Gareth Stevens, 2003.

DiSpezio, Michael A.
Awesome Experiments in Forces and Motion.
Sterling, 2000.

Hammond, Richard.
Can You Feel the Force?
DK Children, 2006.

Lafferty, Peter.
Force and Motion.
DK Children, 1999.

Nankivell-Aston, Sally, and Dorothy Jackson.
Science Experiments with Simple Machines.
Schholastic Library Publishing, 2006.

Smith, Alastair, et al.
Energy, Forces and Motion.
Internet-Linked Library of Science (series)
EDC Publishing 2002.

VanCleave, Janice.
Janice VanCleave's Machines: Mind-boggling Experiments You Can Turn Into Science Fair Projects.
Spectacular Science Projects (series)
Jossey-Bass, 1993.

Web Sites

Fear of Physics
www.fearofphysics.com/
Learn more about gravity, position,
velocity, acceleration, and other topics

From Apples to Orbits—the Gravity Story
library.thinkquest.org/27585/
Well-designed site on the history
and science of gravity

Sport Science
www.exploratorium.edu/sports/
Explore the science behind sports,
including skateboards, surfing, and baseball

All Science Fair Projects
www.all-science-fair-projects.com/
    category57.html
Some suggestions for science fair
projects involving forces and motion

Publisher's note to educators and parents:
Our editors have carefully reviewed these
Web sites to ensure that they are suitable for
children. Many Web sites change frequently,
however, and we cannot guarantee that a
site's future contents will continue to meet
our high standards of quality and educa-
tional value. Be advised that children
should be closely supervised whenever they
access the Internet.

INDEX